PRESIDENTIAL LIBRARIES™

GEORGE BUSH
PRESIDENTIAL LIBRARY

Amy Margaret

The Rosen Publishing Group's
PowerKids Press
New York

For Benjamin Luke

Acknowledgement: The author would like to thank David Ferrell of the George Bush Presidential Library for his invaluable assistance on this project.

Published in 2004 by The Rosen Publishing Group, Inc.
29 East 21st Street, New York, NY 10010

First Edition

Editor: Joanne Riethoff
Book Design: Maria E. Melendez

Photo credits: All images courtesy of the George Bush Presidential Library.

Margaret, Amy.
George Bush Presidential Library / Amy Margaret.— 1st ed.
    v. cm. — (Presidential libraries)
Includes bibliographical references and index.
Contents: A visit to the library and museum — The president as a child — George Bush goes to war — The road to the presidency — Presidential highlights — The first lady — Family man — After the White House.
ISBN 0-8239-6273-3 (lib. bdg.)
1. George Bush Presidential Library and Museum–Juvenile literature. 2. Bush, George, 1924– —Archives—Juvenile literature. 3. Presidents—United States—Archives—Juvenile literature. 4. Bush, George, 1924– —Museums—Texas—College Station—Juvenile literature. 5. Bush, George, 1924– —Juvenile literature. 6. Presidents—United States—Biography—Juvenile literature. [1. George Bush Presidential Library and Museum. 2. Bush, George, 1924– 3. Presidents.] I. Title.
E838.5.B879 M37 2003
973.928'092—dc21

2002000097

Manufactured in the United States of America

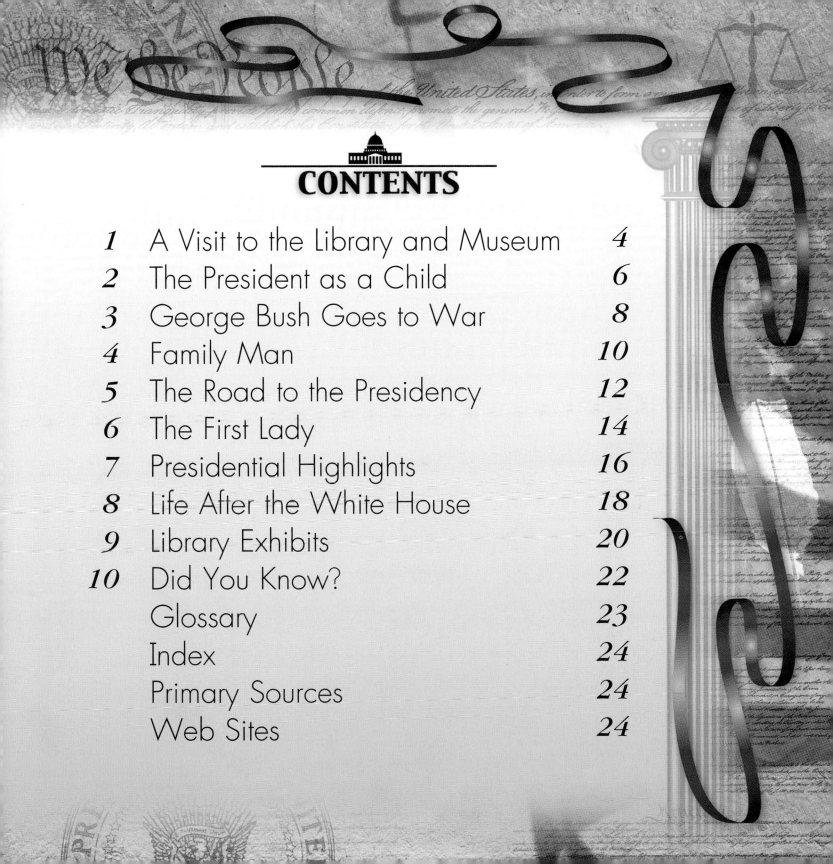

CONTENTS

A VISIT TO THE LIBRARY AND MUSEUM

The Berlin Wall is a symbol of the cold war, which was a time in history when the United States competed with Russia in a struggle for power. This section of the Berlin Wall is on display at the Bush library and museum. It is 12 feet (4 m) high, 4 feet (1 m) wide, and weighs 2 ½ tons (2 t). The cold war ended in 1989, during George Bush's second term as vice president.

The George Bush Presidential Library is in College Station, Texas, at Texas A&M University. George Bush had visited the university twice during his presidency and was warmly welcomed. Bush served as U.S. president from 1989 to 1993. The library opened in 1997. The Fords, the Carters, the Clintons, Lady Bird Johnson, and Nancy Reagan joined George and Barbara Bush to celebrate this day.

The library contains George Herbert Walker Bush's personal and political papers. The museum section is filled with items from Bush's life and objects important to the time period.

The George Bush Presidential Library keeps about 38 million pages of documents and personal papers on Bush's life. It also keeps papers from Bush's vice president, Dan Quayle. All 10 presidential libraries are run by the National Archives and Records Administration (NARA).

On display at the Bush library and museum is this 1947 Studebaker. This car is identical to the car that the Bushes drove across the country when they moved to Odessa, Texas, in 1948. The car was a gift from Chaplain S. Wayland and Betty Hartsfield. It was restored by B. B. Holland.

THE PRESIDENT AS A CHILD

George and his family had maids, a cook, and a chauffeur, or driver. George is shown here with his sister, Nancy, in a photo taken about 1927 or 1928. Their father, Prescott, came from a wealthy family. Even though the family didn't need to worry about money, Dorothy, George's mother, was still very careful with their spending.

On June 12, 1924, George Bush was born in Milton, Massachusetts, outside of Boston. He was the second of five children. He grew up in Greenwich, Connecticut. The family spent summers in Kennebunkport, Maine. The children fished, swam, and sailed. At the library, there is a 1925 film showing George as a baby, taking his first steps at the family's home in Kennebunkport.

George went to high school at Phillips Academy, located in Andover, Massachusetts. It is one of the oldest and most respected schools on the East Coast. His grades were average, but he was involved in several sports and various activities.

Even in high school, George was a leader. He was elected president of his senior class and served as captain of his soccer and baseball teams. George *(bottom left)* is pictured here with the Andover baseball team. This picture was taken during spring training in 1942.

This picture was taken around 1937, and it shows, from left to right, Dorothy (mother), George, Nancy (sister), Jonathan (brother), and Prescott (father). George's older brother, Prescott Jr., was away at school when this picture was taken, and Bucky, another younger brother, wasn't born yet.

GEORGE BUSH GOES TO WAR

George Bush received the Distinguished Flying Cross for his bravery when his plane was hit by the Japanese. In all, he took part in 58 battles and spent 1,228 hours in the air. In the picture above, you can see the medals that Bush received during his time in the U.S. Navy.

When the United States entered **World War II** in 1941, George was still attending school. His parents wanted him to go to college. George wanted to become a naval pilot.

He graduated in 1942. On the day he turned 18 years old, George joined the U.S. Navy. A year later, he officially became a pilot.

On September 2, 1944, George was flying in Japanese territory when his plane was hit. He **parachuted** out of the plane and landed in the ocean. He pulled a life raft from his pack. He sat in the raft for many hours. A U.S. **submarine** picked him up. In December 1944, he was sent home from the war.

This display features the time that Bush spent in the Navy during the war. The plane strung up over the top of the display is a copy of the plane that Bush flew.

This is a letter that Bush wrote to his family on September 3, 1944. Bush is describing what happened on the day that his plane was hit by the Japanese.

Bush is shown here in a TBM Avenger aircraft. This is the kind of plane that he flew during the war.

FAMILY MAN

After returning from the war, George Bush married Barbara Pierce on January 6, 1945. While George Bush worked in the oil business, Barbara Bush raised five children, George W., John Ellis (called Jeb), Neil, Marvin, and Dorothy.

George and Barbara Bush's second child, Robin, sadly died in 1953. She was only three years old when she died of leukemia, a kind of **cancer** that sometimes affects children.

In 1966, the family moved to Washington, D.C. George Bush was elected to the **House of Representatives**. By 1975, the Bush family had lived in 29 homes in 17 cities.

The president lives in the White House, but where does the vice president live? Until 1974, the vice presidential family did not have an official home. Congress ordered that a house at the U.S. Naval Observatory in Washington, D.C., become the vice presidential home. The house was built in 1893, and has 33 rooms! George and Barbara Bush were the second vice presidential family to move into the home.

This photo of George Bush sitting with his wife and children was taken in Houston, Texas, in 1964. From left to right, Marvin, George Bush, Dorothy, Jeb, Barbara, Neil, and George W.

THE ROAD TO THE PRESIDENCY

Once World War II ended, George Bush went to Yale University. He graduated in about three years with a degree in **economics**. In 1948, he, Barbara, and George W. moved to Texas. Bush wanted to get a job without help from his father.

Bush was in the oil business but then decided to get into politics. In 1964, he ran for the **Senate** and lost. He won a place in the House of Representatives in 1966 and in 1968. Bush continued to serve the **Republican** party, working for presidents Nixon and Ford. He served as vice president to Ronald Reagan from 1980 to 1989. Then, in 1990, he ran for president and won.

George was interested in the oil business. After he moved to Texas in 1948, he began to sell oil supplies. He then started to dig for oil and natural gas. Eventually Bush decided to get into politics. This picture of George Bush talking to a man in front of oil machinery was used in his 1964 Senate campaign.

When Bush ran for the Senate in Texas in 1964, it was the first major election in which he had ever run. By Texas standards, he did very well. Texas was largely a Democratic state in the 1960s. This is a picture that Bush used in his campaign for Senator of Texas.

THE FIRST LADY

Barbara Pierce was born on June 8, 1925. She and her family lived in Rye, New York. She is related to the fourteenth U.S. president, Franklin Pierce, who served from 1853 to 1857.

Barbara Bush's special project was **literacy**. In 1966, she became involved with the Reading Is Fundamental (RIF) project. In 1989, the First Lady founded the Barbara Bush Foundation for Family Literacy, which raises money to help families learn to read and write.

The exhibit on Barbara shows how she has helped with literacy. It also has bookshelves with children's stories, along with a couch. Parents can sit and read to their children right in the museum!

The First Lady did many interesting things while in the White House. In 1990, Barbara Bush wrote Millie's Book: As Dictated to Barbara Bush. Millie was the Bushes' dog. Barbara gave the money that she received for the book to the Barbara Bush Foundation. Above: Barbara poses on the Truman Balcony of the White House with Millie for a picture for Good Housekeeping magazine on April 10, 1990.

A major goal of the Barbara Bush Foundation has been to "help every family . . . understand that the home is the child's first school, that the parent is the child's first teacher, and that reading is the child's first subject." Top: Barbara reads to a few children in the White House residence. Bottom: Shown here is the display at the Bush Library. You can see the couch where parents and children can read together.

PRESIDENTIAL HIGHLIGHTS

One of the duties of the president of the United States is to serve as the commander in chief of the military. During a war, this job is very important.

The **Persian Gulf War** started in August 1990, when President Bush sent U.S. troops to Saudi Arabia to protect the country from Iraq. Iraqi president Saddam Hussein had invaded Kuwait and had threatened Saudi Arabia. The United States and its **allies** bombed targets in Iraq and in Kuwait for several weeks. The land battle, called Desert Storm, lasted for about 100 hours. The war ended on April 6, 1991, when the countries signed a **cease-fire**.

One of the most interesting gifts given to President Bush is a 100-year-old door, from the people of Kuwait. People in Kuwait believe that if a man gives you a door to his house, you become a member of his family. The Gulf War began when Iraq invaded Kuwait. Along the door's edge are the names of the Americans who were killed during the war. It is on display at the George Bush Presidential Library.

This exhibit is dedicated to the Gulf War. During this war, 425,000 American troops and 118,000 troops from allied countries were sent to Saudi Arabia, Iraq, and Kuwait.

LIFE AFTER THE WHITE HOUSE

George and Barbara Bush are both active in public service. To inspire others, the George Bush Presidential Library Foundation came up with the George Bush Award (above). This award recognizes people who are serving others at the local, the state, or even the worldwide level.

After George Bush lost the 1994 presidential election to Bill Clinton, he and Barbara made their home in Houston, Texas. Bush decided not to participate in politics any longer. He did **campaign** for his son George W. in 2000 when he ran for president and won.

Recently Bush and his wife have raised nearly $30 million for various causes. Bush is involved with the M. D. Anderson Cancer Center, one of the leading cancer research hospitals in the world. George and Barbara Bush are both involved with the National Dialogue on Cancer. This is a group of cancer organizations that have come together with the goal of cutting cancer deaths in half by 2010.

In recent years, Bush has become active in his church. Bush has served on the vestry, which is a group of leaders in the Episcopal church, at his church in Texas and in Maine. Left: *St. Ann's Episcopal Church in Kennebunkport, Maine, is where the Bushes worship when they visit there.* Right: *George and Barbara Bush pray while at Camp David on January 13, 1991.*

LIBRARY EXHIBITS

The George Bush Library features many exhibits that the other presidential libraries don't have. There is a copy of the office President Bush used at **Camp David**. One unique room is about the Bushes' love of laughter. It shows a video called "Bushes Unplugged" and shows appearances of Bush and his wife in commercials and comedy shows, such as *Saturday Night Live*.

Another display shows a sample from the library's collection of 1,200 elephant figures. These figures were given to the library by Doris Hankamer in 1994. She collected elephants all through her life. Elephants symbolize the Republican party.

There is a section in the library and museum dedicated to temporary exhibits. One of these exhibits was called The White House Garden. *Visitors could take a look at photographs of one of the United States's most historic gardens.*

The White House gardens are among the most photographed and visited landscapes in the world. The gardens are also the presidential family's backyard!

This is an exhibit showing the inside of Air Force One, the presidential plane. This exhibit was created using the aircraft's actual blueprints.

DID YOU KNOW?

Here are some fun facts to share with your friends about the forty-first president of the United States:

Bush is **allergic** to bee stings.

Bush reads *Horseshoe News Digest*. He's played the game horseshoes since childhood.

In July 1985, Bush acted as president for about eight hours while President Reagan was under **anesthesia**.

Bush loves to listen to country western music, especially the Oak Ridge Boys.

Bush, who represented the Republican party, asked President Nixon to **resign** after the **Watergate scandal**. He did this in a letter to Nixon written in August 1974.

When the Bushes first moved to Texas in 1948, they had trouble finding a place to live. Housing in western Texas was so tight that all they could find was a small apartment on a dirt road. In this apartment, they even had to share a bathroom with their neighbor!

GLOSSARY

allergic (uh-LER-jik) Having a bad reaction to something.

allies (A-lyz) Countries that are friendly and that help each other in times of crisis.

anesthesia (a-nus-THEE-zhuh) Medication that makes feeling and pain go away.

campaign (kam-PAYN) A plan to achieve a specific result, such as with an election.

Camp David (KAMP DAY-vid) A place of retreat for the current U.S. president and anyone he wants to invite.

cancer (KAN-ser) A disease in which cells keep growing but do not work properly.

cease-fire (SEES-fyr) A military order to stop fighting.

economics (eh-kuh-NAH-miks) The study of production and supply and demands of goods or services.

House of Representatives (HOWS UV reh-prih-ZEN-tuh-tivs) A part of Congress, the law-making body of the U.S. government.

literacy (LIH-teh-reh-see) Being able to read and write.

parachuted (PAYR-uh-shoot-ed) Jumped from a plane, wearing a device that helps you to land safely.

Persian Gulf War (PUHR-zhin GULF WOR) The war fought in Iraq between Iraq and the United States and its allies from 1990 to 1991.

Republican (rih-PUH-blih-kuhn) Referring to one of the major political parties in the United States.

resign (rih-ZYN) To step down from a position.

Senate (SEH-nit) A law-making part of the U.S. government.

submarine (SUHB-muh-reen) A boat that moves underwater.

Watergate scandal (WAH-tur-gayt SKAN-dul) The upset that happened when officials from the Republican party broke into the Democratic headquarters to steal secrets that would help President Nixon win reelection.

World War II (WURLD WOR TOO) A war fought between the United States, Great Britain, and Russia, and Germany, Japan, and Italy from 1939 to 1945.

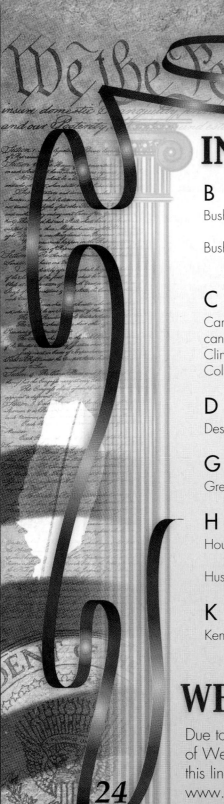

INDEX

PRIMARY SOURCES

All photos were obtained directly from the George Bush Presidential Library.

WEB SITES

Due to the changing nature of Internet links, PowerKids Press has developed an online list of Web sites related to the subject of this book. This site is updated regularly. Please use this link to access the list:
www.powerkidslinks.com/pl/gblm/